Dominus Est—It Is the Lord!

Dominus Est—It Is the Lord!

❀❀❀ ❀❀❀

REFLECTIONS OF A BISHOP OF CENTRAL ASIA ON HOLY COMMUNION

Most Reverend
ATHANASIUS SCHNEIDER

Preface by
Most Reverend Malcolm Ranjith

Translated by
Reverend Nicholas L. Gregoris

NEWMAN HOUSE PRESS

Dominus Est—It Is the Lord!
ISBN 978-0-9778846-1-2

Translation and additional text copyright © 2008
Newman House Press
601 Buhler Court, Pine Beach, NJ 08741
All rights reserved

Contents

Publisher's Foreword   7

Preface *by Most Reverend Malcolm Ranjith*   13

1. "Eucharistic" Women and Holy Communion
   in the Soviet Underground   19

2. "*Cum amore ac timore*": Some Preliminary
   Observations   26

3. The Attitude of Reverence   28

4. The Testimony of the Fathers of the Church   34

5. The Testimony of the Early Church   37

6. The Testimony of the Magisterium   40

7. The Testimony of Liturgical Rites   42

8. The Testimony of the Eastern Churches   44

9. The Testimony of the Protestant Communities   46

10. Conclusion   49

APPENDIX: Glossary of Names   53

Notes   61

Publisher's Foreword

The January 8, 2008, issue of *L'Osservatore Romano,* the daily newspaper of the Vatican, got the attention of the Catholic world with an article by a bishop from Karaganda. The topic had been considered off-limits in most ecclesiastical circles; that the daily of the Holy See would re-visit the subject and thus appear to endorse the research and conclusions of the author could have a "chilling effect" on contemporary liturgical life, according to some commentators. As the story unfolded, we learned that the article was merely a synopsis of a book and that the book had been published by none other than the Libreria Editrice Vaticana, the Vatican Press. The theme of the project was that Communion-in-the-hand and standing for Communion were not consonant with the two-millennia-long Catholic tradition and that both practices need to be re-evaluated for the good of the Church.

When that article made its debut, I immediately made contact with its author, Bishop Athanasius Schneider, and asked if *The Catholic Response*, a periodical published under the auspices of the Priestly Society of the Venerable John Henry Cardinal Newman (as is Newman House Press itself), could produce an English translation of the piece. Bishop Schneider enthusiastically supported the effort, which, in turn, led to an invitation by him and Libreria Editrice Vaticana that Newman House Press publish the full-length book as well. The result is now before the reader.

This work is critically important at this particular juncture of ecclesiastical life, as can be gleaned from the fact that the preface has been written by the secretary of the Congregation for Divine Worship and the Discipline of the Sacraments, Archbishop Malcolm Ranjith, along with an endorsement from the prefect of that dicastery, Francis Cardinal Arinze. One cannot help but wonder if Bishop Schneider's article and book did not play a part in the decision of Pope Benedict XVI to return to the traditional mode of Communion distribution at his Masses, namely, on the tongue to kneeling communicants.

When Communion-in-the-hand was being proposed (and practiced illicitly) in the mid-1960s, the argument was proffered that this was merely a return to the "ancient" usage of the Church, one that would enhance the faith-life of the Church. With the publication of *Memoriale Domini* in 1967, it was abundantly clear that Pope Paul VI did not accept such a view, nor did the world-wide episcopate, who resoundingly opposed any change in the method of Communion distribution. Mysteriously, though, the door was opened for the change. That change was slow in coming to the United States, as the episcopal conference repeatedly rejected proposals for Communion-in-the-hand. Eventually, in 1977, by a slim majority of the bishops, the practice was approved and went into effect on the Solemnity of Christ the King. The materials given parish priests for the catechesis of the faithful were historically flawed and totally one-sided. The "fruits" of the practice are hardly edifying, as polls continue to document loss of Eucharistic faith, even among regular Mass-goers—let alone reports of stolen or desecrated hosts, not a few of which find their way into Satanic Masses.

Thirty years later, Bishop Schneider's book comes to the rescue, as real history and theology combine to demonstrate the genuine Catholic tradition of the universal Church—both East and West. Indeed, the change of the centuries-old practice of priests placing the Sacred Host directly onto the tongue of recipients came precisely from the Protestant Reformers, who were intent on calling into question both the ministerial priesthood and the doctrine of transubstantiation, as their own writings attest. Could one suppose that the re-emergence of the practice would not produce similar confusion and doubts about the very same teachings? In point of fact, it has.

The present work, however, is not limited to an exploration of remote historical texts. The author begins his work by introducing us to three "Eucharistic" women, as he terms them—all known to him personally, two of them being his own mother and his grand-aunt. He describes, in moving and edifying language, how devout Catholics prayed for the Holy Eucharist, waiting longingly for the arrival of a priest. His description puts one in mind of a similar one presented by Pope John Paul II in his first Holy Thursday letter to priests, in which he recounted how the faithful in such situations would gather in an abandoned shrine or church, place a stole on the altar, and recite all the words of the Sacred Liturgy, but halt in silence "at the moment that corresponds to the transubstantiation" as a sign of how "ardently they desire to hear the words that only the lips of a priest can efficaciously utter." Of such a mind and heart were these women of Bishop Schneider's acquaintance in the Soviet Underground, who served as conduits of the Holy Eucharist. In much less dire circumstances, noted Pope Benedict XVI during his 2008 visit to Australia, were lay people who fulfilled a like function: "Our thoughts turn in particular to those settler families to whom Father Jeremiah O'Flynn entrusted the Blessed Sacrament at his departure, a 'small flock' which cherished and preserved that precious treasure, passing it on to the succeeding generations who raised this great tabernacle to the glory of God."

In no way would either Bishop Schneider or Pope Benedict countenance an unwarranted recourse to extraordinary ministers of Holy Communion; indeed, they would agree with Pope John Paul II in condemning such a practice as "reprehensible." And surely, no honest reader can use the lives of these women to advance a campaign for the ordination of women. In reality, the "Eucharistic" women of this book had such a profound love for the Blessed Sacrament, the sacred priesthood, and the Tradition of the Church, that they would have recoiled from any such thoughts. These were lay women who prayed daily that their extraordinary apostolate would end as quickly as possible, with priests able to fulfill their sacred ministry. I hasten to mention that the stories of these women resonated very strongly with me because my own grand-uncle, ordained but three weeks in Ukraine, was martyred by the Bolsheviks, who then confiscated the family farm. The deportees of Central Asia faced the same fate some years later, but their devotion to the Holy Eucharist and their fidelity to the Church saw them through those dark days. We need the same convictions today to withstand the attacks of a militant secularism, which may not threaten to kill our bodies but which does every bit as much harm to our souls, often because the attacks are far more subtle and thus far more dangerous. Keeping the Eucharist in clear relief is the antidote to such a poison.

Finally, some acknowledgments are in order. I wish to say first what a pleasure it has been to work with Bishop Schneider, a kindly gentleman with a faith-filled and priestly heart; even across three continents and an ocean, we have been able to communicate and collaborate effectively out of a love born of a common concern for a renewed sense of the sacrality of the Holy Eucharist. I wish to thank Libreria Editrice Vaticana for the confidence it has placed in Newman House Press by consigning the English edition to our care, as they also did with Father Giovanni Velocci's *Preghiera in Newman* (published by us as *Prayer in Newman*). Likewise, I gratefully note that this translation has been effected through the literary skills of Father Nicholas Gregoris, who was also responsible for *Prayer in Newman*. His passionate devotion to the Blessed Sacrament made this more than a task to be accomplished; rather, he saw it as a labor of love. I also wish to offer a word of thanks to Mr. William Mahoney for adding a set of eyes to the editorial process and for producing the Glossary, found at the end of the book, which should serve as a handy guide for readers unfamiliar with various historical personages and events mentioned in the body of the text.

It is the prayerful hope of each one of us involved in this project that this effort will bear much fruit in returning the Church of the West to that deep and abiding awareness that in every Eucharistic encounter, *Dominus Est—It is the Lord!* And may our external actions always reflect that interior conviction.

Reverend Peter M. J. Stravinskas
Publisher and Editor

Preface

In the Book of Revelation, St. John recounts how having seen and heard that which was revealed to him, he prostrated himself in adoration at the feet of the angel of God (Rev 22:8). To prostrate oneself or to kneel down before the majesty of the divine presence, in humble adoration, was a habit of reverence that Israel always practiced in the presence of the Lord. The First Book of Kings says: "Now as Solomon finished offering all this prayer and supplication to the Lord, he arose from before the altar of the Lord, where he had knelt with hands outstretched toward heaven; and he stood, and blessed all the assembly of Israel with a loud voice" (1 Kings 8:54–55). The position of supplication of the king is clear: He was kneeling before the altar.

The same tradition can also be found in the New Testament, where we see Peter kneeling before Jesus (see Lk 5:8); Jairus, who knelt to request the healing of his daughter (Lk 8:41); the Samaritan who returned and knelt to give thanks to Jesus (Lk 17:16); and Mary, the sister of Lazarus, who, on her knees, asked the favor of having her brother brought back to life (Jn 11:32). The same attitude of prostration before the stupendous presence and divine revelation is found throughout the Book of Revelation (Rev 5:8, 14; 19:4).

Intimately linked to this tradition was the conviction that the holy Temple of Jerusalem was the dwelling place of God and, therefore, in the Temple one had to exhibit bodily gestures expressive of a profound sense of humility and reverence in the presence of the Lord.

Likewise, in the Church, the profound conviction that in the Eucharistic Species the Lord is truly and really present and the growing practice of keeping Holy Communion in tabernacles contributed to the practice of kneeling in an attitude of humble adoration before the Lord in the Eucharist.

In fact, concerning the Real Presence of Christ in the Eucharistic Species, the Council of Trent proclaimed that "in the Blessed Sacrament of the Eucharist, after the consecration of the bread and wine, our Lord Jesus Christ, true God and man, is truly, really and substantially contained under the appearances of those perceptible realities" (DS 1651).

Besides, St. Thomas Aquinas had already defined the Eucharist as *latens Deitas** (*Hymns*). And the faith in the Real Presence of Christ in the Eucharistic Species was already part of the essence of the Faith of the Catholic Church and an intrinsic part of Catholic identity. It was clear that no one could edify the Church if such faith was even minimally under attack.

Therefore, the Eucharist, bread transubstantiated into the Body of Christ and wine into the Blood of Christ, God in our midst, had to be received with awe, with the greatest reverence, and in an attitude of humble adoration. Pope Benedict XVI, recalling the words of Saint Augustine: "*Nemo autem illam carnem manducat, nisi prius adoraverit; peccemus non adorando*" (No one eats that flesh without first adoring it; we should sin were we not to adore it; *Enarrationes in Psalmos* 89, 9), underscores that history: "Receiving the Eucharist means adoring him whom we receive. . . . Only in adoration can a profound and genuine reception mature" (*Sacramentum Caritatis* no. 66).

Following this tradition, it is clear that assuming gestures and attitudes of the body and the spirit that facilitate silence, recollection, and humble acceptance of our poverty

---

* Literally; "hidden Godhead" (i.e., "Godhead in hiding").

before the infinite greatness and holiness of the One Who comes to meet us in the Eucharistic Species became consistent and indispensable. The best way to express our sense of reverence toward the Eucharistic Lord was to follow the example of Peter, who, as the Gospel recounts, threw himself on his knees before the Lord and said: "Depart from me, for I am a sinful man, O Lord" (Lk 5:8).

Now, it is observed in some churches how those responsible for the liturgy not only force the faithful to receive the Holy Eucharist standing but have also removed all the kneelers, thus forcing the faithful to remain seated or standing, even during the elevation of the Sacred Species presented for adoration. It is strange that such provisions have been made in dioceses by liturgical officials or in churches by pastors, without the least amount of consultation of the faithful, even though, today more than ever, there is talk in many places of "democracy in the Church."

At the same time, speaking of Communion-in-the-hand, it is necessary for all to recognize that the practice was introduced as an abuse, and hurriedly, in many places within the Church right after the Council, that it changed the centuries-long earlier practice, and that it is becoming now a regular practice throughout the whole Church. This change was justified by asserting that it better reflected the Gospel or the ancient practice of the Church.

It is true that if it is possible to receive on the tongue, one can also receive on the hand, both being bodily organs of equal dignity. Some people, to justify Communion-in-the-hand, cite the words of Jesus: "Take and eat" (Mk 14:22; Mt 26:26). Yet, whatever the reasons put forth to sustain this practice, we cannot ignore what happens at the practical level when this method is used. This practice contributes to a gradual, growing weakening of the attitude of reverence toward the Sacred Eucharistic Species. The earlier practice, on the other hand, better safeguards the sense of reverence.

Instead, an alarming lack of recollection and an overall spirit of carelessness have entered into liturgical celebrations. One now sees communicants frequently returning to their places as though nothing extraordinary has happened. Even more, children and adolescents are distracted. In many instances, one does not find that sense of seriousness and interior silence which ought to signal the presence of God in the soul.

Then there are the abuses of those who take the Sacred Species off to keep as a souvenir, of those who sell the Hosts, or, worse yet, of those who take them for the purpose of profaning them in satanic rituals. Such situations have been observed. Furthermore, in large concelebrations, even in Rome, on various occasions one finds the Sacred Species tossed on the ground.

This situation causes us to reflect on the grave loss of faith, but also on the outrages and offenses to the Lord, Who deigns to come to meet us, wishing to make us like unto Him, so that the holiness of God may be reflected in us.

The Pope speaks of the necessity not only of our understanding the true and profound significance of the Eucharist, but also of celebrating the liturgy with dignity and reverence. He mentions that it is necessary to be aware of the importance of "gestures and posture, such as kneeling during the moments following the Eucharistic Prayer" (*SC* no. 65). Furthermore, in speaking of the reception of Holy Communion, he invites all to "do all possible so that the gesture in its simplicity correspond to the value of the personal encounter with the Lord Jesus in the Sacrament" (no. 50).

Against this background, one can appreciate this little book written by His Excellency Monsignor Athanasius Schneider, auxiliary bishop of Karaganda in Kazakhstan, from its very significant title: *Dominus Est*. It is to be hoped that this work will contribute to the current discussion on the Eucharist, the real and substantial presence of Christ in the consecrated Species of Bread and Wine. It is significant that Bishop Schneider begins his presentation on a personal note, recalling the profound Eucharistic faith of his mother and two other women, a faith preserved amid the great sufferings and sacrifices that the tiny community of Catholics of that country endured in the years of the Soviet persecution. Starting from his experience, which aroused in him a great faith, wonder, and devotion for the Lord present in the Eucharist, he presents us with an historical-theological *excursus* that clarifies how the practice of receiving Holy Communion on the tongue, while kneeling, became the normative practice in the Church for a long period of time.

I think it is now time to evaluate carefully the practice of Communion-in-the-hand and, if necessary, to abandon what was actually never called for in the Vatican II document *Sacrosanctum Concilium* nor by the Council Fathers but was, in fact, "accepted" after it was introduced as an abuse in some countries. Now, more than ever, it is necessary to help the faithful renew a living faith in the Real Presence of Christ in the Eucharistic Species in order to strengthen the life of the Church herself and to defend her in the midst of the dangerous distortions of the Faith, which such a situation continues to cause.

The reasons for such a change ought to be not so much academic as pastoral—spiritual as well as liturgical. In short, it involves taking steps that will better build up the faith of Catholics. In this sense, Bishop Schneider demonstrates praiseworthy courage, because he knows the full meaning of the words of St. Paul: "Let all things be done for edification" (1 Cor 14:26).

+ Malcolm Ranjith
Secretary of the Congregation for Divine Worship and the Discipline of the Sacraments

DOMINUS EST

Christus vincit, Christus regnat, Christus imperat
Christ conquers, Christ reigns, Christ rules

❧❧ ❦❦

(1)

"Eucharistic" Women and Holy Communion in the Soviet Underground

The Soviet Communist regime, which lasted about seventy years (1917–1990), had the pretension of establishing a kind of earthly paradise. But this kingdom could not last, because it was founded on lies, on the violation of the dignity of man, on the denial and even the hatred of God and of His Church. It was a kingdom in which God and spiritual values could not, should not, have any place. Every sign that could remind men of God, of Christ, and of the Church was removed from public life and from the sight of men. Yet there continued to exist a reality that could remind men of God, namely, the priest. Because the priest was a reminder of God, he should not be visible; in fact, he should not even exist.

The persecutors of Christ and His Church considered the priest to be the most dangerous person because, implicitly, they knew that only the priest could give God to men, give Christ in the most concrete and direct manner possible, that is, through the Eucharist and Holy Communion. Therefore, the celebration of the Holy Mass was prohibited.

But no human power could conquer the Divine Power that was at work in the mystery of the Church and, above all, in the sacraments.

During those dark years, the Church, in the immense Soviet empire, was forced to live underground. But the most important thing was this: The Church was alive, indeed very alive, even though she lacked visible structures, even though she lacked sacred buildings, even though there was a tremendous scarcity of priests. The Church was most alive because she did not completely lack the Eucharist, even though it was rarely available to the faithful; because she did not lack souls with solid faith in the Eucharistic Mystery; because she did not lack women—often mothers and grandmothers—with a "priestly" soul who safeguarded and even administered the Eucharist with extraordinary love, with care, and with the greatest reverence possible, in the spirit of the Christians of the first centuries, expressed in the adage *cum amore ac timore* (with love and fear).

Among the numerous examples of "Eucharistic" women in the Soviet Underground there will be presented here the example of three women known personally by the author: Maria Schneider (the author's mother); Pulcheria Koch (sister of the grandfather of the author); Maria Stang (a parishioner of the Diocese of Karaganda).

Maria Schneider, my mother, used to tell me that after the Second World War, the Stalinist regime deported many Germans from the Black Sea and from the Volga River to the Ural Mountains to engage them in forced labor. All of them were interned in the most impoverished barracks in the city ghetto. There were a few thousand German Catholics. Some Catholic priests would go to them in the most secretive manner in order to administer the sacraments, putting their own lives in jeopardy. Among the priests who came most frequently was Father Alexij Saritski, a Ukrainian Greek-Catholic and bi-ritual priest who died a martyr on

October 30, 1963, near Karaganda (he was beatified by Pope John Paul II in 2001). The faithful affectionately called him "God's vagabond." In January of 1958, in the city of Krasnokamsk near Perm in the Ural Mountains, Father Alexij, from his place of exile, suddenly and secretly arrived in the city of Karaganda in Kazakhstan.

Father Alexij worked so that the greatest number of faithful could be prepared for the reception of Holy Communion, making himself available to hear the confessions of the faithful literally day and night, without sleeping and without eating. The faithful begged him, "Father, you must eat and sleep!" But he would reply, "I can't, because the police can arrest me at any moment, and then many people would be left without confession and, therefore, without Communion." After everyone had gone to confession, Father Alexij began to celebrate the Holy Mass. Suddenly, a voice resounded, "The police are coming!" Maria Schneider, who was attending the Mass, said to the priest, "Father, I can hide you; let's flee!" The woman led the priest into a house outside the German ghetto and hid him in a room, also bringing him something to eat, and said: "Father, now you can finally eat and rest a bit; and when it gets dark, we will flee to a nearby city." Father Alexij was sad, because, though all had made their confessions, they could not receive Holy Communion, because the Holy Mass, which had just begun, had been interrupted by the police raid. Maria Schneider said: "Father, all the faithful will make a Spiritual Communion with great faith and much devotion, and we hope that you will be able to return to give us Holy Communion."

With the coming of evening, preparations were made for the flight. Maria Schneider left her two little children (a two-year-old boy and a six-month-old girl) with her mother and called on Pulcheria Koch (the aunt of her husband). The two women took Father Alexij and led him for twelve kilometers through the forest, in the snow and the cold, 30 degrees below zero.[1] The women arrived at a little train station, bought a ticket for Father Alexij, and sat with him in the waiting room; the train was not due for an hour. Suddenly, the door opened. A policeman entered and spoke directly to Father Alexij: "Where are you heading?" The priest was not able to respond, out of fear—not for his own life, but for the life and fate of the young mother, Maria Schneider. The young woman herself responded to the policeman: "This is our friend, and we are accompanying him. Look, here is his ticket," and she handed the ticket over to the policeman. The policeman, looking at the ticket, told the priest: "Please do not enter the last car, because it will be dislodged from the rest of the train at the next station. *Bon voyage!*" The policeman exited the waiting room. Father Alexij looked at Maria Schneider and said, "God has sent us an angel! I will never forget what you have done for me. If God will permit it, I will return to give all of you Holy Communion, and in my every Mass I will pray for you and your children."

After a year, Father Alexij was able to return to Krasnokamsk. This time he could celebrate the Holy Mass and give Holy Communion to the faithful. Maria Schneider asked him a favor: "Father, could you leave me a consecrated Host because my mother is gravely ill and wants to receive Communion before dying?" Father Alexij left a consecrated Host, on condition that Holy Communion be administered to the woman with the greatest possible respect. Maria Schneider promised to act in this way. Before moving with her family to Kirghistan, Maria administered Holy Communion to her sick mother. In order to do this, Maria put on new white gloves and with a tweezers gave Holy Communion to her mother. Afterwards, she burned the envelope in which the consecrated Host had been kept.

The families of Maria Schneider and Pulcheria Koch later moved to Kirghistan. In 1962, Father Alexij secretly visited Kirghistan and found Maria and Pulcheria in the city of Tokmak. He celebrated Holy Mass in the house of Maria Schneider and, another time, in the house of Pulcheria Koch. Out of gratitude to Pucheria, this old woman who had helped him escape in the darkness and cold of winter in the Ural Mountains, Father Alexij left her a consecrated Host, giving this precise instruction: "I leave you a consecrated Host. Practice the devotion in honor of the Sacred Heart of Jesus on the First Friday for nine consecutive months. Every First Friday of the month, expose the Blessed Sacrament in your house, inviting for adoration persons who are absolutely trustworthy, with everything carried out in the greatest secrecy. After the ninth month, you must consume the Host, but do so with great reverence!" And so was it done. For nine months, there was clandestine Eucharistic Adoration at Tokmak. Maria Schneider was also among the female worshipers.

Kneeling before a little Host, all the adoring women, these truly Eucharistic women, ardently desired to receive Holy Communion. But, unfortunately, there was only a little Host and at the same time many people who desired to receive Holy Communion. For this reason, Father Alexij had decided that at the end of the nine months only Pulcheria would receive Holy Communion, with the other women making a Spiritual Communion. Nevertheless, these Spiritual Communions were very precious, because they rendered these "Eucharistic" women capable of transmitting to their children, as if with their maternal milk, a profound faith and great love for the Eucharist.

The entrustment of this little consecrated Host to Pulcheria Koch in the city of Tokmak in Kirghistan was the last pastoral action of Blessed Alexij Saritski. Immediately after his return to Karaganda from his missionary journey in Kirghistan, in April of 1962, Father Alexij was arrested by the secret police and placed in the concentration camp of

Dolinka, near Karaganda. After much mistreatment and humiliation, Father Alexij obtained the palm of martyrdom *ex aerumnis carceris* (from the sufferings of prison) on October 30, 1963. His liturgical memorial is celebrated on this day in all the Catholic churches of Kazakhstan and Russia; the Ukrainian Greek-Catholic Church celebrates it together with other martyrs on June 27. He was a Eucharistic saint, who could educate Eucharistic women. These Eucharistic women were like flowers that grew up in the darkness and desert of a clandestine existence, thus keeping the Church truly alive.

The third example of a "Eucharistic" woman is that of Maria Stang, a German woman from Volga, deported to Kazakhstan. This saintly mother and grandmother had a life full of incredible sufferings and continual renunciations and sacrifices. However, she was a person full of faith, hope and spiritual joy. Already from childhood, she desired to dedicate her life to God. On account of the Communist persecution and deportation, her pilgrimage of life was filled with sorrow. Maria Stang writes in her memoirs: "They took away the priests. In the nearby village, there was still a church but, unfortunately, there was no longer a priest there, nor the Blessed Sacrament. But without the priest, without the Blessed Sacrament, the church was so cold. I had to cry bitterly." From that moment, Maria began to pray every day and to offer sacrifices to God with this prayer: "O Lord, give us a priest again, give us Holy Communion! I suffer all things willingly for love of You, O Most Sacred Heart of Jesus!" In the vast place of deportation in the eastern part of Kazakhstan, Maria Stang secretly used to gather together other women in her house every Sunday to pray. During these Sunday gatherings, the women often cried and prayed: "Mary, our most holy and dearest Mother, see how poor we are. Give us again priests, teachers and shepherds!"

From 1965 on, Maria Stang traveled once a year to Kirghistan, where a Catholic priest was living in exile (a distance of more than a thousand kilometers). In the vast villages of eastern Kazakhstan, German Catholics had not seen a priest for already more than twenty years. Maria writes: "When I arrived at Frunse (today Bishkek) in Kirghistan, I found a priest. Entering his house, I saw the tabernacle. I had not been able to imagine that in my lifetime I would be able to see once more the tabernacle and the Eucharistic Lord. I knelt down and began to cry. Afterwards, I drew closer to the tabernacle and kissed it." Before Maria Stang left for her village in Kazakhstan, the priest handed over to her a pyx with some consecrated Hosts. The first time that the faithful gathered together in the presence of the Blessed Sacrament, Maria said to them: "We have a joy and happiness that no one can imagine: We have with us the Eucharistic Lord, and we can receive Him." Those present responded: "We cannot receive Holy Communion because we have not gone to confession for so many years." Afterwards, the faithful held a council and made the following decision: "Since the times are most difficult and the Blessed Sacrament has already been brought to us from over a thousand kilometers away, God will be merciful toward us. Let us place ourselves spiritually in the confessional before the priest. We will make a perfect act of contrition, and each one of us will impose an individual penance." Everyone acted accordingly, and then all received Holy Communion on their knees and in tears. They were tears at one and the same time of penitence and of joy.

For thirty years, Maria Stang gathered the faithful together for prayer each Sunday, teaching catechism to the children and the adults, preparing couples for the Sacrament of Matrimony, carrying out the Rites of Burial and, above all, administering Holy Communion. Every time she distributed Holy Communion, she did so with an ardent heart and a reverential fear. She was a woman with a truly priestly soul, a "Eucharistic" woman.

(2)

"Cum amore ac timore"—Some Preliminary Observations

(a) Pope John Paul II, in his last encyclical, *Ecclesia de Eucharistia*, gave the Church an ardent admonition that resounds like a veritable testament:

> By giving the Eucharist the prominence it deserves, and by being careful not to diminish any of its dimensions or demands, we show that we are truly conscious of the greatness of this gift. We are urged to do so by an uninterrupted tradition, which from the first centuries on has found the Christian community ever vigilant in guarding this "treasure." Inspired by love, the Church is anxious to hand on to future generations of Christians, without loss, her faith and teaching with regard to the mystery of the Eucharist. There can be no danger of excess in our care for this mystery, for "in this sacrament is recapitulated the whole mystery of our salvation" (no. 61).

Knowledge of the greatness of the Eucharistic mystery is demonstrated particularly by the way in which the Body of the Lord is distributed and received. This appears evident in the rite of Communion, inasmuch as it constitutes the consummation of the Eucharistic Sacrifice. For the faithful, this is the culminating point of the encounter and of personal union with Christ, really and substantially present under the humble veil of the Eucharistic Species. This moment of the Eucharistic Liturgy has a truly eminent importance that brings with it a special pastoral demand in the ritual aspect of gesture as well.

(b) Aware of the greatness of the moment of Holy Communion, the Church in her two-millennia–long tradition has searched to find a ritual expression that can bear witness in the most perfect manner to her faith, love, and respect. This is verified when, in the wake of an organic development, stemming from at least the sixth century, the Church began to adopt the method of distributing the Sacred Species of the Eucharist directly into the mouth. This is attested to in several places: in the biography of Pope Gregory the Great and an indication by the same Pope relative to Pope Agapitus.[2] The Synod of Cordoba in 839 condemned the sect of so-called "Casiani" because of their refusal to receive Holy Communion directly into their mouths.[3] Then the Synod of Rouen in 878 confirmed the norm in force regarding the administration of the Lord's Body on the tongue, threatening sacred ministers with suspension from their office if they distributed Holy Communion to the laity on the hand.[4]

In the West, the gesture of prostration and genuflection before reception of the Body of the Lord was observed in monastic settings already from the sixth century (e.g., in the monasteries of St. Columban).[5] Later, in the tenth and eleventh centuries, this gesture was even more widespread.[6]

At the end of the patristic age, the practice of receiving Holy Communion directly into the mouth became thenceforth an almost universal practice. This organic development may be considered a fruit of the spirituality and Eucharistic devotion stemming from the time of the Fathers of the Church.

In fact, there are several exhortations from the Fathers of the Church about the very great reverence and concern for the Eucharistic Body of the Lord, particularly regarding fragments of the consecrated Bread. When it began to be observed that conditions no longer existed to assure the requirements for respect and for the highly sacred character of the Eucharistic Bread, the Church both in the East and in the West, in an admirable consensus and almost instinctively, perceived the urgency of distributing Holy Communion to the laity only in the mouth.

The noted liturgist Joseph Jungmann explains that, with Communion distributed directly into the mouth, various concerns were eliminated: the need for the faithful to have clean hands; the even graver concern that no fragment of the consecrated Bread be lost; the necessity of purifying the palm of the hand after reception of the Sacrament. The Communion cloth and, later, the Communion plate would be an expression of heightened regard for the Sacrament of the Eucharist.[7]

This development has been equally advanced by a growing deepening of faith in the Real Presence, expressed in the West, for example, through the practice of adoration of the Most Blessed Sacrament solemnly exposed.

(3)

The Attitude of Reverence

The Eucharistic Body and Blood are the gift *par excellence* that Christ has left for the Church, His Bride. Pope John Paul II speaks in the encyclical *Ecclesia de Eucaristia* of the "wonder and adoration before the unsurpassable gift of the Eucharist" (no. 48), which must be made manifest even in external gestures: "With this heightened sense of mystery, we understand how the faith of the Church in the mystery of the Eucharist has found historical expression not only in the demand for an interior disposition of devotion, but also *in outward forms* meant to evoke and emphasize the grandeur of the event being celebrated" (no. 49).

And so, the attitude more consonant with this gift is the attitude of receptivity, the attitude of the humility of the centurion, the attitude of one who allows himself to be fed, precisely the attitude of a child. This is likewise expressed in the following words of a Eucharistic hymn: "The bread of angels becomes the bread of men . . . Oh, what a marvelous thing: the poor and humble servant eats the Lord!"[8]

The word of Christ, which invites us to receive the Kingdom of God like a child (see Lk 18:17), can find its illustration in that very beautiful and impressive manner of receiving the Eucharistic Bread directly into one's mouth and on one's knees. This ritual manifests in an opportune and felicitous way the interior attitude of a child who allows himself to be fed, united to the gesture of the centurion's humility and to the gesture of "wonder and adoration."

Pope John Paul II demonstrated the need for external expressions of respect toward the Eucharistic Bread:

> Though the idea of a "banquet" naturally suggests familiarity, the Church has never yielded to the temptation to trivialize this "intimacy" with her Spouse by forgetting that he is also her Lord and that the "banquet" always remains a sacrificial banquet marked by the blood shed on Golgotha. *The Eucharistic Banquet is truly a "sacred" banquet*, in which the simplicity of the signs conceals the unfathomable holiness of God: *O sacrum convivium, in quo Christus sumitur!* The bread which is broken on our altars, offered to us as wayfarers along the paths of the world, is *panis angelorum*, the bread of angels, which cannot be approached except with the humility of the centurion in the Gospel: "Lord, I am not worthy to have you come under my roof" (Mt 8:8; Lk 7:6) (*Ecclesia de Eucharistia*, no. 48).

The attitude of a child is the truest and most profound attitude of a Christian before his Savior, Who nourishes him with His Body and Blood, according to the following moving expressions of Clement of Alexandria: "The *Logos* is everything for the child, father and mother and tutor and nurse. 'Eat my flesh,' He says, 'and drink my blood!' . . . O amazing mystery!"[9]

One can suppose that during the Last Supper Christ would have given the bread to each apostle directly in the mouth and not only to Judas Iscariot (see Jn 13:26–27). In fact, there existed a traditional practice in the Middle East of Jesus' time that continues even to our own day, by which the head of the house feeds his guests with his own hand, placing a symbolic piece of bread into the mouths of the guests.

Another biblical consideration is furnished from the account of the call of the prophet Ezekiel. He symbolically receives the Word of God directly into his mouth: "'Open your mouth, and eat what I give you.' And when I looked, behold, a hand was stretched out to me, and, lo, a written scroll was in it. . . . So I opened my mouth, and he gave me the scroll to eat. . . . Then I ate it; and it was in my mouth as sweet as honey" (Ez 2:8–9; 3:2–3).

In Holy Communion, we receive the Word-made-Flesh— made Food for us little ones, for us children. And so, when we approach Holy Communion, we can remind ourselves of this gesture of the prophet Ezekiel or of the word of Psalm 81:11, which one finds in the Liturgy of the Hours on the Solemnity of Corpus Christi: "Open your mouth, and I will fill it" (*dilata os tuum, et implebo illud*).

Christ truly nourishes us with His Body and Blood in Holy Communion and, in the patristic era, this is likened to a mother's nursing, as shown in these evocative words of St. John Chrysostom: "Now see how intimately Christ has been united to His Spouse [the Church]; see with what food He satisfies us. He Himself is our food and nourishment; and just as a woman nourishes her child with her own blood and milk, Christ also constantly nourishes with His own Blood those to whom He has given birth [by Baptism]." [10]

The gesture of an adult who kneels and opens his mouth so as to be fed like a child corresponds in a felicitous and impressive manner to the admonitions of the Fathers of the

Church concerning the attitude to have during Holy Communion, that is to say, *cum amore ac timore* (with love and fear).[11]

The typical gesture of adoration is the biblical one of kneeling, as received and practiced by the first Christians. For Tertullian, who lived between the second and third centuries, the highest form of prayer is the act of adoration of God, which ought to manifest itself also in the gesture of genuflection: "The angels likewise all pray; every creature prays; cattle and wild beasts pray and bend their knees."[12]

St. Augustine warned that we sin if we do not adore the Eucharistic Body of the Lord when we receive It: ". . . no one eats that flesh without first adoring It. . . . We should sin were we not to adore It."[13]

In an ancient *Ordo Communionis* (Order of Communion) in the liturgical tradition of the Coptic Church, it was established: "Let all prostrate on the ground, small and great, and then they will begin to distribute Communion."[14]

According to the *Mystagogical Catecheses*, attributed to St. Cyril of Jerusalem, the faithful ought to receive Communion with a gesture of adoration and veneration: "Do not stretch out your hands, but, bowing low in a posture of worship and reverence. . . ."[15]

St. John Chrysostom exhorts those who approach the Eucharistic Body of the Lord to imitate the Magi from the East in a spirit and gesture of adoration:

> Let us draw nigh to Him then with fervency and with inflamed love. . . . This Body, even lying in a manger, Magi reverenced. Yea, men profane and barbarous, leaving their country and their home, both set out on a long journey, and when they came, with fear and great trembling worshiped Him. Let us, then, at least imitate those Barbarians, we who are citizens of heaven. For they indeed when they saw Him but in a manger, and in a hut, and no such thing was in sight as you behold now, drew

nigh with great awe; but you behold Him not in the manger but on the altar, not a woman holding Him in her arms, but the priest standing by, and the Spirit with exceeding bounty hovering over the gifts set before us. You do not see merely this Body itself as they did, but you know also Its power, and the whole economy, and art ignorant of none of the holy things which are brought to pass by It, having been exactly initiated into all.[16]

Already in the sixth century, in the Greek and East Syrian churches, a triple prostration was prescribed as one approached to receive Holy Communion.[17]

On the intimate link between adoration and Holy Communion, Cardinal Joseph Ratzinger spoke very evocatively:

Eating it [the Eucharist]—as we have just said—is a spiritual process, involving the whole man. "Eating" it means worshiping it. Eating it means letting it come into me, so that my "I" is transformed and opens up into the great "we," so that we become "one" in him (see Gal 3:16). Thus adoration is not opposed to Communion, nor is it merely added to it. No, Communion only reaches its true depths when it is supported and surrounded by adoration.[18]

And so, before the humility of Christ and His love, communicated to us in the Eucharistic Species, adoration is not possible without bending the knee. Cardinal Ratzinger again observed: "kneeling is the right, indeed the intrinsically necessary gesture" before the living God.[19] In the Book of Revelation, the book of the heavenly liturgy, the gesture of prostration of the twenty-four ancient ones before the Lamb can be the model and standard for how the Church on earth should treat the Lamb of God when the faithful approach Him in the Sacrament of the Eucharist.[20] The liturgical norms of the Church do not require a gesture of adoration for those receiving Holy Communion while kneeling, since the fact of kneeling in and of itself already is a gesture of adoration. However, those who communicate while standing must first make a gesture of reverence, that is, of adoration.[21]

Mary, the Mother of the Lord, is the model of the interior and exterior attitude of how to receive the Body of the Lord. At the moment of the Incarnation of the Son of God, she showed the greatest receptivity and humility: "Behold, the handmaid of the Lord." The exterior gesture most consonant with this attitude is that of kneeling (as one finds not infrequently in the iconography of the Annunciation). The model of the loving adoration of the Virgin Mary "should inspire us every time we receive Eucharistic communion," said Pope John Paul II.[22] The moment of receiving the Eucharistic Body of the Lord is certainly the most suitable occasion for the faithful, in this earthly life, to externalize the interior attitude as one "bows low in adoration and in unbounded love."[23]

Blessed Pope John XXIII spoke in a similar way: "Blessed Julian Eymard left behind a writing in which he states that by following Jesus one never leaves Mary and her beautiful title of Our Lady of the Blessed Sacrament." Furthermore, he wrote: "We all kneel, like children following the example of their good mother, before the great mystery of love of her blessed Son, Jesus."[24]

The method of distributing Holy Communion—at times not sufficiently appreciated for its importance—in reality is vested with important significance and has consequences for the faith and devotion of the faithful, inasmuch as it visibly mirrors the faith, the love and the care with which the Church treats her Divine Spouse and Lord present in the humble species of bread and wine.

The awareness that in the humble Eucharistic Species is really present the entire majesty of Christ, King of Heaven, before Whom all the angels prostrate, was most alive in the times of the Fathers of the Church. Among so many voices, it is enough to cite the following moving exhortation of St. John Chrysostom:

> And why speak I of the world to come? Since here this mystery makes earth become to you a heaven. Open only for once the gates of heaven and look in; nay, rather not of heaven, but of the heaven of heavens; and then you will behold what I have been speaking of. For what is there most precious of all, this will I show you lying upon the earth. For as in royal palaces, what is most glorious of all is not walls, nor golden roofs, but the person of the king sitting on the throne; so likewise in heaven the Body of the King. But this, you are now permitted to see upon earth. For it is not angels, nor archangels, nor heavens and heavens of heavens, that I show you, but the very Lord and Owner of these.[25]

(4)

The Testimony of the Fathers of the Church

The Fathers of the Church demonstrated a lively concern that no one lose the smallest particle of Eucharistic Bread, as St. Cyril of Jerusalem exhorted in this very impressive manner:

> . . . take care to lose no part of It [the Body of the Lord]. Such a loss would be the mutilation of your own body. Why, if you had been given gold-dust, would you not take the utmost care to hold it fast, not letting a grain slip through your fingers, lest you be so much the poorer? How much more carefully, then, will you guard against losing so much as a crumb of that which is more precious than gold or precious stones?"[26]

Already Tertullian (d. ca. 220) had given witness to the Church's anxiety and sorrow should even a fragment be lost: "We feel pained should any wine or bread, even though our own, be cast upon the ground."[27]

The extreme care and veneration for the fragments of the Eucharistic Bread was a phenomenon characteristic of the Christian communities of the third century and known to Origen: "You are accustomed to take part in the divine mysteries, so you know how, when you have received the Body of the Lord, you reverently exercise every care lest a particle of It fall, and lest anything of the consecrated gift perish. You account yourselves guilty, and rightly do you so believe, if any of it be lost through negligence." [28]

St. Jerome was concerned with the thought that a Eucharistic fragment could fall to the ground, a possibility he considered worrisome and a spiritual danger. "When we go to the mysteries—one who is faithful understands this—if anything should fall to the ground, there is danger." [29]

In the liturgical tradition of the Coptic Church one finds the following warning: "There is no difference between the smaller and larger particles of the Eucharist, even those smallest ones which cannot be perceived with the naked eye; they deserve the same veneration and possess the same dignity as the whole Bread."

In some Eastern Liturgies, the consecrated Bread is designated by the name "pearl." Thus the *Collectiones canonum Copticae* (Coptic Collections of Canons) reads: "God forbid that any of the pearls or consecrated fragments should adhere to the fingers or fall to the ground!" [30]

In the tradition of the Syrian Church, the Eucharistic Bread was compared with the fire of the Holy Spirit. There was a living consciousness of faith in the presence of Christ in even the smallest fragments of the Eucharistic Bread, as St. Ephrem attests: "Jesus filled up the Bread with Himself and the Spirit and called It His living Body. That which I have now given you, says Jesus, do not consider bread, do not trample underfoot even the fragments. The smallest fragment of this Bread can sanctify millions of men and is enough to give life to all who eat It." [31]

The extreme vigilance and care of the Church of the first centuries lest any fragment of the Eucharistic Bread be lost was a universally diffused phenomenon: Rome (see Hippolytus, *Traditio apostolica*, 32); North Africa (see Tertullian, *De corona*, 3, 4); Gaul (see Caesarius of Arles, *Sermo* 78, 2); Egypt (see Origen, *In Exodum hom.*, 13, 3); Antioch and Constantinople (see John Chrysostom, *Ecloga quod non indige accedendum sit ad divina mysteria*); Palestine (see Jerome, *In Psalmos*, 147, 14); Syria (see Ephrem, *In Hebdomada Sancta*, 4, 4).

In a time when Communion was distributed only on the tongue and a communion plate was used, Pope Pius XI ordered that the following stringent exhortation be published:

> In the administration of the Eucharistic Sacrament, one must demonstrate a particular zeal, so that no fragments of the consecrated Hosts be lost since in each particle is present the entire Body of Christ. Therefore, one should take the greatest care that fragments do not easily separate from the Host and fall to the ground, where—*horribile dictu!*—they could become mixed with the garbage and be trampled underfoot.[32]

In a moment of great importance in the life of the Church, such as the sacramental reception of the Body of the Lord, one must show a corresponding care, vigilance, and attention. Pope John Paul II, speaking about the reception of Holy Communion, noted that "cases of a deplorable lack of respect towards the Eucharistic Species have been reported, cases which are imputable not only to the individuals guilty of such behavior but also to the pastors of the church who have not been vigilant enough regarding the attitude of the faithful towards the Eucharist."[33] For this reason, one must take into account the particular and historical circumstances of the communicants, so that nothing would occur that could bring about damage as regards this sacrament, as Saint Thomas Aquinas admonished.[34] Every sacrament possesses a double and inseparable character: the cult of divine adoration and the salvation of man.[35] The form of the rite must therefore guarantee, in as secure a way as possible, respect for the Eucharist and for its sacred character.

It was pecisely this aspect of the unity between the interior disposition and its manifestation in exterior gestures that Blessed Columba Marmion explained with impressive words full of the fervor of the Faith. Thus did he pray to the Eucharistic Jesus: "Lord Jesus, for love of us, in order to draw us to You, to become our Food, You veil Your majesty. But You will lose nothing of our homage thereby. The more You hide Your Divinity the more we wish to adore You, the more too we wish to cast ourselves at Your feet with profound reverence and ardent love."[36]

Blessed Columba Marmion explains the reason for the exterior veneration of the Eucharistic Species, starting with the prayer of the Church: "O Lord, give us the grace to *venerate* the sacred mysteries of Your Body and Your Blood." Why venerate? Because Christ is God, because the reality of the Sacred Species is a sacred and divine reality. He Who hides Himself in the Eucharist is He Who, with the Father and the Holy Spirit, is infinite Being, the Omnipotent: "O Christ Jesus, really present upon the altar, I cast myself down at Your feet; may all adoration be offered to You in the Sacrament which You left to us on the eve of Your Passion, as the testimony of the excess of Your love!"[37]

(5)

The Testimony of the Early Church

In the Early Church, the faithful, before receiving the consecrated Bread, had to wash the palms of their hands.[38]

Moreover, the faithful bowed profoundly, receiving the Body of the Lord into the mouth directly from the right hand and not from the left.[39] The palm of the hand served as a kind of paten or corporal, especially for women. Thus one reads in a sermon of St. Caesarius of Arles (470–542): "When they desire to communicate, all men wash their hands, and all women show their splendid garments[40] when they receive the Body of Christ."[41] Customarily, the palm of the hand was purified or washed after the reception of the Eucharistic Bread, as is still the norm for the Communion of clerics in the Byzantine Rite.

The Early Church was careful that the reception of the Body of the Lord on the hand would be accompanied by an external attitude of profound adoration, as can be determined from the following homily of Theodore of Mopsuestia: "Each of us approaches, paying the adoration due, and thus making a profession of faith that one is receiving the Body of the King. You, however, after receiving the Body of Christ in your hands, adore Him with great and sincere love, fix your gaze on Him, and kiss Him."[42]

In the ancient canons of the Chaldean Church, even the celebrating priest was forbidden to place the Eucharistic Bread into his own mouth with his fingers. Instead, he had to take the Body of the Lord from the palm of his hand and, with that, place It directly into his mouth; the reason for this was to signify that he was dealing here not with ordinary food but with a heavenly food: "The priest," we read in the Canon of John Bar-Abgari, "is directed to receive the particle of consecrated Bread directly from the palm of his hand. He may not place It with his hand into his mouth, but must take It with his mouth, for this concerns a heavenly food."[43]

In the Chaldean and Syro-Malabar Rites, a particular rubric expresses the profound respect rendered in handling the consecrated Bread: Before the priest in the Eucharistic Liturgy touches the Body of the Lord with his fingers, his hands are incensed. Cardinal Ratzinger made the following observation: The fact that the priest takes the Body of the Lord himself not only distinguishes him from the laity, but must also impel him to be aware of finding himself before the *mysterium tremendum* and of acting in the person of Christ.[44]

That a mortal man may take the Body of the Lord directly into his own hands demands a great spiritual maturity, according to St. John Chrysostom: "[Since the priest] constantly handles the common Lord of all, tell me what rank shall we give him? What great purity and what real piety must we demand of him? For consider what manner of hands they ought to be which minister in these things."[45]

In the ancient Syriac Church, the rite of Communion distribution was compared to the scene of the purification of the Prophet Isaiah by the seraph. In one of his sermons, St. Ephrem puts these words on Christ's lips:

> The coal carried [by the seraph] cleansed the lips of Isaiah. It is I Who, carried now to you by means of bread, have sanctified you. The tongs which the Prophet saw and with which the coal was taken from the altar, were the figure of Me in the great Sacrament. Isaiah saw Me, as you see Me now extending My right hand and carrying to your mouths the living Bread. The tongs are My right hand. I take the place of the seraph. The coal is My Body. All of you are Isaiah.[46]

This description allows one to conclude that, in the Syriac Church at the time of St. Ephrem, Holy Communion was distributed directly into the mouth. This can also be determined from the Liturgy of St. James, which was even more ancient than that of St. John Chrysostom. In the Liturgy of St. James, before distributing Holy Communion to the faithful, the priest recites this prayer: "The Lord will bless us, and make us worthy with the pure touchings of our fingers to take the live coal, and place it upon the mouths of the faithful for the purification and renewal of their souls and bodies, now and always." [47]

In the West Syrian Rite, in distributing Communion, the priest recites this formula: "May the propitious and enlivening coal of the Body and Blood of the Lord our God be given to the faithful for the pardon of offenses and for the remission of sins."

There exists a similar witness from St. John Damascene: "Let us draw near to it with an ardent desire. . . and partake of the divine coal, . . . that we may be inflamed and deified by the participation in the divine fire. Isaiah saw the coal. But coal is not plain wood but wood united with fire: in like manner also the bread of the Communion is not plain bread but bread united with divinity." [48]

Based on the experience of the first centuries, in the organic growth in theological comprehension of the Eucharistic mystery and its consequent ritual development, the manner of distributing Communion on the hand was limited by the end of the patristic era to a specific group, namely, the clergy, as is still the case with the Eastern rites. The Eucharistic Bread began to be distributed to the laity—intincted in the consecrated Wine in the Eastern rites—directly into the mouth. In the Eastern rites, only the non-consecrated bread is distributed on the hand, the so-called *antidoron*.[49] Thus is shown in a clear manner the difference between Eucharistic Bread and bread that is merely blessed.

VI.

The Testimony of the Magisterium

Some years ago, Cardinal Joseph Ratzinger made the following disturbing observation regarding Communion time in certain places: "By going to Communion without 'discernment,' we fail to reach the heights of what is taking place in Communion; we reduce the Lord's gift to the level of everyday ordinariness and manipulation."[50]

These words of then-Cardinal Ratzinger closely echo the warnings of the Fathers of the Church regarding the moment of Communion, as we can see through the example of the following expressions of St. John Chrysostom, called Doctor of the Eucharist:

> Do you consider how much holiness you must possess when you have received signs greater than the Jews received in the Holy of Holies? To dwell within you, in fact, you do not have the Cherubim, but the Lord of the Cherubim; you do not have the ark or the manna or the tablets of stone or the rod of Aaron, but the Body and Blood of the Lord—the spirit rather than the letter—you have an unutterable gift. And so, with so many even greater signs and more venerable mysteries that you have been honored, for how much greater holiness are you held to account.[51]

The authentic and strict link uniting the early (patristic) era with the Church of today in these matters is the reverent care for the Body and Blood of the Lord, even in the smallest fragments.[52]

In a recent instruction for the Eastern Catholic Churches on the method of distributing Communion (especially on the practice of having only priests touch the Eucharistic Bread), the Holy See expresses a criterion that is valid for the liturgical praxis of the whole Church: "Even if this excludes enhancing the value of other criteria, also legitimate, and implies renouncing some convenience, a change of the traditional usage risks incurring a non-organic intrusion with respect to the spiritual framework to which it refers."[53]

To the extent that a culture exists that is alienated from

the faith and unknowing of the One before Whom it ought to kneel, the liturgical gesture of kneeling "is the right, indeed the intrinsically necessary gesture," observed Cardinal Ratzinger.[54]

Pope John Paul II insisted on the fact that, in light of the secularized culture of modernity, the Church of today must feel a special obligation toward the sacredness of the Eucharist:

> This must always be remembered, perhaps above all in our time, when we see a tendency to do away with the distinction between the "sacred" and "profane," given the widespread tendency, at least in some places, to desacralize everything. In view of this fact, the Church has a special duty to safeguard and strengthen the sacredness of the Eucharist. In our pluralistic and often deliberately secularized society, the living faith of the Christian community—a faith always aware of its rights vis-à-vis those who do not share that faith—ensures respect for this sacredness.[55]

(7)

The Testimony of Liturgical Rites

Through the rite itself, the Church attests to her faith in Christ and adores Him Who is present in the Eucharistic Mystery and Who comes as food given to the faithful.[56] The method of handling the Eucharistic Bread holds a highly pedagogical value. The rite must be a faithful witness to what the Church believes and must be the pedagogue at the service of the faith, at the service of the dogma. Liturgical gesture, in a preeminent way the gesture of receiving the Eucharistic Body of the Lord, of receiving in fact the "Holy of Holies," imposes on the body and the soul attitudes proper to the demands of the spirit.

The Servant of God, Cardinal John Henry Newman, taught in this way:

> To believe, and not to revere, to worship familiarly, and at one's ease, is an anomaly and a prodigy unknown even to false religions, to say nothing of the true one. Not only the Jewish and Christian religions, which are directly from God, inculcate the spirit of "reverence and godly fear," but those other religions which have existed, or exist, whether in the East or the South, inculcate the same. Worship, forms of worship—such as bowing the knee, taking off the shoes, keeping silence, a prescribed dress, and the like—are considered as necessary for a due approach to God.[57]

St. John Chrysostom rebuked priests and deacons who distributed Holy Communion out of human respect and without the proper care: "Nay, though it be from ignorance that he come to communicate, forbid him, be not afraid. Fear God, not man. If thou shouldst fear man, thou wilt be left to scorn even by him, but if God, thou wilt be an object of respect even to men. . . . I would give up my life rather than impart of the Lord's Blood to the unworthy; and will shed my own blood rather than impart of such awful Blood contrary to what is meet."[58]

St. Francis of Assisi admonished clerics, calling them to a particular vigilance and reverence in the distribution of Holy Communion:

> Now, let all who administer mysteries of so holy a nature, and especially those who minster thoughtlessly, give their careful consideration. . . . and [those who] administer it without due concern. . . . And all this does not move us with loving concern, though Our Lord is loving enough to entrust Himself to our hands, and we handle Him and receive Him on our lips day after day! Do we not know that we are destined to get into His hands?[59]

Nor should we forget the always relevant admonition of the Roman Catechism conveying the basic teaching of the Apostle Paul in 1 Corinthians 11:27–30:

> As of all the sacred mysteries bequeathed to us by our Lord and Savior as most infallible instruments of divine grace, there is none comparable to the most holy Sacrament of the Eucharist; so, for no crime is there a heavier punishment to be feared from God than for the unholy or irreligious use by the faithful of that which is full of holiness, or rather which contains the very author and source of holiness.[60]

(8)

The Testimony of the Eastern Churches

Nowadays, the Church of the Latin Rite could learn a great deal from the Eastern Churches about the way one must treat the Eucharistic Christ during Communion, to cite only one of the many beautiful witnesses: "The Holy One goes forth onto the diskos[61] and into the chalice, in glory and majesty, accompanied by priests and deacons, in a grand procession. Thousands of angels and servants, filled with the fire of the Spirit, go forth before the Body of Our Lord, glorifying It."[62]

The axiom of the Fathers of the Church concerning the way to treat Christ during Communion was this: *cum amore ac timore* (with love and fear)! These moving words of St. John Chrysostom, Doctor of the Eucharist, also bear witness to this axiom: "And with fitting modesty, as if approaching the King of the Heavens, receiving this holy and immaculate Victim, let us kiss Him, and embracing Him with our eyes, let us inflame our mind and our soul, lest we incur judgment and damnation . . . , so that we render ourselves holy and edify our neighbors."[63]

The Eastern Churches have maintained this interior attitude, as well as this external attitude, even up until the present. The famous Russian writer Nikolay Gogol, in his little work *Meditations on the Divine Liturgy*,[64] commented on the moment of receiving Holy Communion in this way:

> With ardent desire, inflamed by the fire of the holy love for God, those about to receive Communion draw near, reciting the profession of faith in the Crucified Lord. After the recitation of that prayer, each one no longer approaches the priest, but the flaming Seraph. The faithful open their mouths to receive from the holy spoon the burning charcoal of the Body and Blood of Christ.[65]

A modern saint of the Russian Orthodox Church, a priest by the name of John of Kronstadt (d. 1908), thus describes the spiritual aspect of the moment of Holy Communion, along with the gestures appropriate to it: "What would happen, O my Lord God, Jesus Christ, if You made the light of Your divinity to shine from Your most holy Sacrament, when the priest brings It in his hands to a sick person? Before this light, all who would encounter It or see It would fall prostrate on the ground spontaneously, just as the angels cover their faces before this Sacrament. While, on the other hand, so many treat this heavenly Sacrament with indifference!"[66]

In an explanation of the Divine Liturgy, recently edited by the Russian Orthodox Church, one finds the following instruction given to the faithful who communicate: "Those lay faithful who are prepared to receive the Sacred Mysteries, after the exclamation of the deacon,[67] must approach the chalice with the fear of God; because they are approaching fire, they must approach with faith in the Sacrament and with love for Christ. Each one must prostrate on the ground, adoring Christ truly present in the Sacred Mysteries."[68]

The Early Church and the Fathers of the Church demonstrated a great sensibility for the significance of ritual gesture. That is why the primary and continuous effect of the sacred and liturgical rite consists in distancing and liberating man from the mundane.[69]

(9)

The Testimony of Protestant Communities

The authentic spirit of Eucharistic devotion of the Church Fathers developed organically at the end of antiquity in the whole Church, East and West, in the corresponding ways of receiving Holy Communion in the mouth, preceded by prostration on the ground (in the East) or with kneeling (in the West). In this context, it is instructive to compare the development of the rite of Communion in the Protestant communities. In the first Lutheran communities, Communion was received in the mouth and kneeling, for Luther did not deny the Real Presence. On the other hand, Zwingli, Calvin, and their successors, who denied the Real Presence, introduced, already in the sixteenth century, Communion given on the hand and standing: "Standing and moving for Communion was customary."[70] A similar practice was observed in the communities of Calvin in Geneva: "It was the custom to move and stand to receive Communion. People stood at the table and took up the elements with their own hands."[71]

Some synods of the Calvinist Church of Holland, in the sixteenth and seventeenth centuries, established formal bans on receiving Communion kneeling: "Very early, the people might have knelt during the prayer [Lord's Supper] and also received Communion kneeling but . . . several synods forbade this in order to avoid any suggestion that the bread was being venerated."[72]

In the consciousness of Christians of the second millennium (whether Catholic or Protestant), the gesture of receiving Communion standing or kneeling was not a matter of indifference. In some diocesan editions of the *Rituale Romanum* after the Council of Trent, the ancient practice of giving the faithful the non-consecrated wine as an ablution for the mouth was preserved. In those instances, it was prescribed that the faithful would not receive the wine kneeling but standing.[73]

Furthermore, one must take account of the highly pedagogical value of a sacral and reverential gesture. A commonplace gesture has no pedagogical effect that could help increase the sense of the sacred. It must be recognized how little capability modern man has for a liturgical or sacred act, as Romano Guardini correctly and prophetically observed in an article written in 1965: "The man of today is not capable of a liturgical act. For this action, it is not enough to have instruction or education; no, initiation is needed, which at root is nothing but the performance of the act." [74]

If every liturgical celebration is a sacred action *par excellence* (see *Sacrosanctum Concilium*, no. 7), that must also be the case, and especially so, for the rite of receiving Holy Communion. Pope Benedict XVI, in his post-synodal apostolic exhortation *Sacramentum Caritatis*, emphasized the sacrality of Holy Communion: "Receiving Holy Communion means adoring him whom we receive" (no. 66).

The attitude of adoration toward Him Who is truly present under the humble form of a piece of consecrated Bread, not only in His Body and Blood, but also in the majesty of His divinity, is expressed most naturally and obviously through the biblical gestures of adoration—kneeling or prostration. Whenever St. Francis of Assisi saw the belltower of a church, even at a distance, he knelt and adored Jesus present in the Holy Eucharist.

Would it not correspond more to the truth of the intimate reality of the consecrated Bread if the faithful of today in receiving Communion would prostrate themselves on the ground and open their mouths, as the prophet Ezekiel received the Word of God (see Ez 2), allowing themselves to be fed like a child (for Holy Communion is a spiritual nourishment)? Such an attitude has been demonstrated by generations of Catholics in all the churches for almost the entire second millennium. Such a gesture would also be an impressive sign professing faith in the Real Presence of God in the midst of the faithful. If some non-believer happened upon the liturgical action and observed such an act of adoration, perhaps he too, "falling on his face, will worship God and declare that God is really among you" (1 Cor 14:25). This is how the encounters of the faithful with the Eucharistic Christ in the august and holy moment of Communion ought to be.

The famous English convert Frederick William Faber (1814–1863) was pushed to conversion when he witnessed a moving gesture of adoration and faith in the Real Presence of Christ in the Eucharist, in the Basilica of Saint John Lateran in Rome in 1843. For a Catholic, that was an ordinary and common scene, but for Faber, it was a scene he could not forget for his whole life.

He recalls it thus:

> . . . and when Pope Gregory descended from his throne, and knelt at the foot of the altar, and we all knelt with him, it was a scene more touching than I had ever seen before; the red robes of the prostrate cardinals, the purple of the inferior prelates, the soldiers kneeling, and miscellaneous crowd, the magnificence of the stupendous church, *and the invisible presence of its great historic memories,* and in the midst that old man in white, prostrate before the uplifted Body of the Lord, and the dead, dead silence—oh, what a sight it was! (emphasis in original).[75]

(1 0)

Conclusion

Against the background of the two-millennia-long history of piety and liturgical tradition of the universal Church, East and West alike, especially regarding the organic development of the patristic patrimony, we can offer the following summary:

1. The organic development of Eucharistic piety as a fruit of the piety of the Fathers of the Church led all the Churches, both in the East and in the West, already in the first millennium to administer Holy Communion directly into the mouths of the faithful. In the West, at the beginning of the second millennium, there was added the profoundly biblical gesture of kneeling. In the various liturgical traditions of the East, the moment of receiving the Body of the Lord was surrounded by various awe-inspiring ceremonies, often involving a prior prostration of the faithful to the ground.

2. The Church prescribes the use of the paten for Communion to avoid having any particle of the Sacred Host fall to the ground (see *Missale Romanum, Institutio generalis,* no. 118; *Redemptionis sacramentum,* no. 93) and that the bishop wash his hands after the distribution of Communion (see *Caeremoniale episcoporum,* no. 166). When Communion is given on the hand, not infrequently particles separate from the Host, either falling to the ground or remaining on the palm and fingers of the communicants.

3. The moment of Holy Communion, inasmuch as it is the encounter of the faithful with the Divine Person of the Redeemer, demands by its very nature typically sacred gestures such as prostration to the ground. (On Easter morning, the women adored the Risen Lord by prostrating themselves before Him [see Mt 28:9], and the Apostles did

the same [see Lk 24:52], and perhaps the Apostle Thomas as he said, "My Lord and my God!" [Jn 20:28].)

4. Allowing oneself to be fed like a baby by receiving Communion directly into the mouth ritually expresses in a better way the character of receptivity and of being a child before Christ Who feeds us and nourishes us spiritually. An adult, on the other hand, takes the food himself with his fingers and places it into his own mouth.

5. The Church prescribes that during the celebration of Holy Mass, at the Consecration, the faithful must kneel. Would it not be more liturgically proper if, at the moment of Holy Communion when the faithful approach the Lord in a bodily manner as closely as possible, the One Who is the King of Kings, that they would greet Him and receive Him on their knees?

6. The gesture of receiving the Body of the Lord in the mouth and kneeling could be a visible testimony to the faith of the Church in the Eucharistic Mystery and even something that heals and teaches our modern culture, for which kneeling and spiritual childhood are completely foreign phenomena.

7. The desire to offer the august Person of Christ affection and honor at the moment of Holy Communion in a visible manner would correspond to the spirit and example of the bi-millennial tradition of the Church: *Cum amore ac timore* ("with love and fear," the adage of the Fathers of the first millennium) and *quantum potes, tantum aude* ("do as much as you can," the adage of the second millennium, coming from Aquinas's Sequence for Corpus Christi, the *Lauda Sion*).

At the end of this work, let us devote some space to the moving prayer of Maria Stang, German mother and grandmother of the Volga, who was deported to Kazakhstan during Stalin's regime. This woman had a "priestly" heart, guarding the Eucharist and bringing It in the midst of the Communist persecutions to the faithful dispersed throughout the boundless steppes of Kazakhstan. She prayed with these words:

> There, where my dear Jesus dwells,
> where He is enthroned in the tabernacle,
> there I wish to be kneeling continually.
> There, I wish to pray unceasingly.
> Jesus, I love You deeply.
> Hidden Love, I adore You.
> Abandoned Love, I adore You.
> Despised Love, I adore You.
> Love trampled underfoot, I adore You.
> Infinite Love, dying on the Cross for us, I adore You.
> My dear Lord and Savior,
> make it be that I am all love and expiation
> toward the Most Blessed Sacrament
> in the heart of Your most loving Mother Mary. Amen.

God willing, the pastors of the Church will be able to renew the house of God which is the Church, placing the Eucharistic Jesus in the center, giving Him the first place, making it so that He receive gestures of honor and adoration also at the moment of Holy Communion. The Church must be reformed, starting from the Eucharist! *Ecclesia ab Eucharistia emendanda est!* The Church must be reformed by the Eucharist.

The Sacred Host is not some *thing*, but some *One*. "He is there," was the way St. John Mary Vianney synthesized the Eucharistic Mystery. Therefore, we are involved with nothing other than, and no one less great than, the Lord Himself: *Dominus est!* (It is the Lord!).[76]

Glossary of Names

Agapetus, St. (b. ?; d. 536)

Agapetus [Agapitus] was pope from 535 to 536. For his first public act, Agapetus burned a document anathematizing Dioscurus, who had been anathematized by Boniface II on a false charge of simony. Agapetus desired to clear Dioscurus' name and burned the unfounded document in front of the clergy of Rome.

Augustine, St. (354–430)

Aurelius Augustinus Hipponensis was a philosopher, theologian, and bishop of Hippo. He was heavily influenced by Platonism and is noted for having structured the concepts of a just war and of original sin. Augustine's writings were arguably the most influential in the Middle Ages and continue to be influential today. He is known as the Doctor of Grace because of his defense of an orthodox notion of grace and free will.

Basilica of St. John Lateran

The Basilica of St. John Lateran is the official seat (or cathedral) of the Bishop of Rome. Its title in Latin is translated "The Basilica of St. John in the Lateran." The basilica, named after St. John the Baptist and St. John the Evangelist, is located in a section of Rome called the Lateran. One of the four major basilicas in Rome, it alone possesses the title of "ecumenical mother church," that is, the mother church of the entire world.

Caesarius of Arles, St. (b. ca. 468-471; d. ca. 542-543)

Caesarius was the Bishop of Arles—though he is sometimes called Caesarius of Chalon, his place of birth being Chalon-sur-Saône. He was a theologian, administrator, and preacher. Caesarius is best known for his sermons, in which he used simple language and images drawn from scenes of common life, such as the market and the vineyard. His sermons are usually explanations of morality, sin, Purgatory, and Hell.

Calvin, John (b. July 10, 1509; d. May 27, 1564)

John Calvin was a French Protestant who supported the Protestant Reformation. He structured a system of theology, known as Calvinism, that includes an extreme version of predestination, in which men are held to be destined to Heaven or Hell based on divine preordination from all eternity.

Chaldean Church

The Chaldean Church is the name given to those Nestorians who came into full communion with the Bishop of Rome, thus uniting themselves fully with the Catholic Church. The Chaldean Church consists of two groups: the Turco-Persians, called the Chaldeans, and the Indians, called the Christians of St. Thomas or the Syro-Malabar Church. The Chaldeans currently number 600,000 to 700,000 believers, with many having immigrated to the United States, particularly to Michigan, Arizona, and California.

Clement of Alexandria (b. ca. 150; d. ca. 211–216)

Clement of Alexandria belonged to the Catholic Church in Alexandria. He integrated aspects of Greek philosophy with the teachings of Christianity. Clement posited deification as the goal of life and taught a kind of Christian Platonism. He was a prominent figure in the school of Alexandria, which is known for its scholarship and manuscripts of Sacred Scripture.

Columba Marmion, Bl. (1858–1923)

Columba Marmion was a monk and priest. He taught philosophy at Clonliffe Seminary. In 1909, he was made the Abbot of Maredsous, where he died January 30, 1923. Marmion was a zealous monk with a deep interior life. John Paul II beatified him September 3, 2000.

Columban, St. (540–615)

Columbanus [Columban] was an Irish missionary who founded numerous monasteries in Europe and disseminated Celtic penitential practices, including private confession to a priest. His name is Latin for "dove."

Cyril of Jerusalem, St. (b. ca. 313; d. 386)

Cyril of Jerusalem was a priest and theologian, whose most famous works are the twenty-three catechetical lectures he gave as a priest. The letters are practical and filled with pastoral love. They are directed to the neophytes, the newly baptized, and to those preparing to receive Holy Communion. The instructions to this latter group are called *mystagogic* because they deal with the mysteries of the Faith. In 1883, Pope Leo XIII declared Cyril a Doctor of the Church.

Ephrem, St. (b. ca. 306; d. 373)

Ephrem, a deacon in Syria, was a theologian and writer of hymns, poems, and biblical commentaries in the Syrian language. Ephrem's theological works are usually of a practical nature and were intended to edify the Christians of his day. His works represent an early form of Christianity not yet heavily influenced by Western ideas.

Faber, Frederick William (b. June 28, 1814; d. September 26, 1863)

Frederick William Faber was a convert, entering the Roman Catholic

Church at Northampton in 1845. He was ordained a Catholic priest in 1847 and eventually became an Oratorian. He is widely known as a writer of hymns, two of the more famous being "Faith of Our Fathers" and "There's a Wideness in God's Mercy."

Francis of Assisi, St. (b. ca. 1181/1182; d. 1226)

Francis of Assisi was the founder of the Order of Friars Minor (Franciscans). After an injury, he changed the course of his life and followed the evangelical counsels of poverty, chastity, and obedience with intense zeal and in imitation of Christ. The Franciscans were a mendicant order: meaning that they begged for all their material necessities. Francis is probably widely assiciated with his love of all creation, both inanimate and animate.

Gregory the Great, Pope (b. ca. 540; d. March 12, 604)

Gregory the Great was Pope from 590 to 604. He is a prominent figure in the history of the Church, exerting a tremendous influence on her organization and discipline. Two notable effects of his pontificate include: the placing of the "Our Father" before the fractioning of the Host at Mass, and prohibiting deacons from chanting any part of the Mass save the Gospel. A "criticism" leveled against Gregory is that he emptied his treasury by giving to so many charities. He is a Doctor of the Church.

Gregory XVI, Pope (b. September 18, 1765; d. June 1, 1846)

Bartolomeo Alberto Cappellari reigned as Pope Gregory XVI from 1831 to 1846. Prior to his elevation to the papacy, Cappellari was the abbot of San Gregorio monastery in Rome. This connection very likely explains his choice of "Gregory" for his pontifical name. Gregory XVI was deeply traditional. He resisted attempts to modernize and democratize the Papal States and Europe, working rather to strengthen both the spiritual and temporal authority of the papacy.

Gogol, Nikolay (b. March 31, 1809; d. February 21, 1852)

Nikolai Vasilievich Gogol was born in Ukraine and became a prominent author, writing in the Russian language. Some call him the "father of modern Russian realism." Gogol was among the first to criticize Russia's manner of living. Two of his better-known works are *Dead Souls* and *The Inspector-General.*

Guardini, Romano (b. February 17, 1885; d. October 1, 1968)

Roman Guardini was a Catholic priest, professor, and author. He taught at the University of Berlin, the University of Tübingen, and the University of Munich. The Nazis made Guardini resign from the University of Berlin when he criticized their erroneous opinions regarding Jesus Christ and emphasized Jesus' identity as a Jew. His books *The Lord* and *The Spirit of the Liturgy* are still widely read

Hippolytus of Rome, St. (b. ca. 170; d. ca. 236)
Hippolytus of Rome was described by Photius as a disciple of Irenaeus, who was a disciple of Polycarp, who was a disciple of John the Apostle and Evangelist. Hippolytus, as a priest, was a prolific writer in the early Church. He followed the Novatian schism for a time and lived in conflict with the Popes, for which he is sometimes labeled the first Antipope. Hippolytus eventually reconciled with the Catholic Church and died a martyr's death.

Jerome, St. (b. ca. 347; d. 420)
Eusebius Sophronius Hieronymus, or Jerome, was a priest and Christian apologist. He is primarily known for the Vulgate Bible, the translation of the Scriptures from Hebrew and Greek into Latin. Jerome also wrote many letters, homilies, and treatises in defense of the Faith. He is a Doctor of the Church.

John Chrysostom, St. (b. ca. 347; d. 407)
John Chrysostom was the archbishop of Constantinople. His eloquent preaching earned him the title *Chrysostom*, which means "golden-tongued." Chrysostom denounced the abuse of authority in both the political and ecclesiastical realms. He also provided a liturgy that is still in use today in the Greek Church. Chrysostom is a Doctor of the Church.

John Damascene, St. (b. ca. 676; d. ca. 754–787?)
John of Damascus, or John Damascene, was a Syrian priest and monk. He contributed to various Church disciplines including theology, philosophy, law, and music. John wrote works explaining the Faith and composed many hymns still used in Eastern monasteries. He is a Doctor of the Church and is sometimes also called the Doctor of the Assumption because of his writings on the Assumption of Mary into Heaven.

John of Kronstadt (b. October 19, 1829; d. December 20, 1908)
Ivan (John) Ilyich Sergiyev was a Russian Orthodox priest who worked in Kronstadt at Saint Andrew's Cathedral. He belonged to the Alliance of the Russian People, but did not engage in politics. The Russian Orthodox Church canonized him in 1990.

John XXIII, Pope, Bl. (b. November 25, 1881; d. June 3, 1963)
Angelo Giuseppe Roncalli reigned as Pope John XXIII from October 28, 1958, to June 3, 1963. He is best known for convening the Second Vatican Council, (1962–1965), a decision he attributed to an inspiration of the Holy Spirit. He died before the Council's completion. Pope John Paul II beatified him on September 3, 2000, and his feast day was set for October 11, which is the date the first session of the Second Vatican Council began. (Although a Catholic Pope, John

XXIII is remembered liturgically also by the Evangelical Lutheran Church in America on June 3, and the Anglican Church in Canada remembers him on June 4.)

Julian Eymard, St. (b. February 4, 1811; d. August 1, 1878)

Peter Julian Eymard was a priest in France who founded two religious institutes: the Congregation of the Blessed Sacrament and the Servants of the Blessed Sacrament. When the French sculptor Rodin had given up sculpting after his sister's death, Eymard advised Rodin to return to his vocation as an artist. Pope John XXIII canonized Eymard on December 9, 1962.

Jungmann, Joseph (1889–1975)

Joseph Andreas Jungmann was a prominent liturgist of the twentieth century. His works have had a significant influence on the liturgical reforms from the time of the Second Vatican Council to the present. His most famous work, *Missarum Solemnia* (*The Mass of the Roman Rite*), is a detailed history of the Western liturgy.

Liturgy of St. James

Based on the ancient rite of the Church of Jerusalem, the Liturgy of Saint James is the oldest form of the liturgy. It is still substantially followed by the Syriac Orthodox Church and the Indian Orthodox Church. It is associated with James the Just, who is called the "brother" of the Lord and who wrote the Epistle of James in the New Testament.

Luther, Martin (b. November 10, 1483; d. February 18, 1546)

Martin Luther, a German monk and professor, became a reformer who changed the course of Europe by instigating the Protestant Reformation. Luther challenged the authority of the Church and insisted that Scripture alone (*sola scriptura*) was necessary for salvation. He was officially excommunicated at the Diet of Worms in 1521 and never officially reconciled with the Church.

Newman, John Henry (b. February 21, 1801; d. August 11, 1890)

John Henry Newman was an Anglican priest who converted to Roman Catholicism, on October 9, 1845. He was a major leader of the Oxford Movement, which was intended to bring the Church of England back to its Catholic origins. Pope Leo XIII named him a Cardinal on May 12, 1879. The cause for Newman's canonization is under way.

Origen (b. ca. 185; d. ca. 254)

Origen Adamantius was a priest and theologian who taught in Alexandria. He was expelled from the school of Alexandria for being ordained without the permission of the Alexandrian patriarch. Origen made a corrected version of the Septuagint, the Greek version of the Old Testament. He also wrote many commentaries and offered a philosophical exposition of the teachings of Christianity. Origen is not recognized as a saint, most likely because of an overzealous interpretation of Christian morality, which led him to emasculate himself, and in light of some questionable teachings, such as his consideration of a possible final salvation for the demons.

Pius XI, Pope (b. May 31, 1857; d. February 10, 1939)

Ambrogio Damiano Achille Ratti took the name Pius XI and was Pope from February 6, 1922, to February 10, 1939. His papal motto was *Christ's peace in Christ's Kingdom.* He established the Feast of Christ the King and canonized Sir Thomas More and Thérèse of Lisieux. His most famous encyclical, *Quadragesimo Anno,* highlighted the Church's interest in the moral and ethical aspects of economic and social issues. Pius XI was also interested in the participation of lay persons in the Church.

Synod of Cordoba

The Synod of Cordoba [Cordova] of 839 gathered in Spain to condemn the doctrines of a heretical sect known as "Casiani." The sect probably came from Northern Africa. Their heretical doctrines included rejecting the veneration of relics, declaring some foods unclean, insisting on more austere fasts, and demanding that all communicants should be able to receive the Host in their own hands. These and other positions were condemned at this synod.

Synod of Rouen

The Synod of Rouen, France, which met around 878, gave the following directive: "*nulli autem laico aut feminae eucharistiam in manibus ponat, sed tantum os eius*" (the Eucharist may never be placed in the hands of a lay man or woman, but only in the mouth).

Syriac (language)

Syriac was once a major spoken and literary language used throughout the Middle East. It was an Eastern Aramaic language, disseminating both culture and Christianity throughout Asia. It was eventually replaced by Arabic, on which it exerted a significant influence.

Syro-Malabar Rite

The Syro-Malabar Rite is one of the 22 Eastern Catholic Churches in full communion with the Catholic Church. Syro-Malabar Catholics are also called the Christians of St. Thomas because they trace their origins to St. Thomas the Apostle, who they believe came to India in the year 52. The Church was formerly called the Syro-Chaldean Church; in Kerala, India, members of the Rite are called Syrian Catholics.

Tertullian (b. ca. 160; d. ca. 220)

Quintus Septimius Florens Tertullianus was a prolific Christian writer and the first to write Christian literature in Latin. Tertullian was an apologist and wrote against various heresies. His most notable contribution to theology is probably his use of the Latin term *trinitas,* from which we derive the term "Trinity." Tertullian was also the first to give an exposition of the term. He is not officially counted among the saints because he ended his life subcribing to the heresy of Montanism.

Theodore of Mopsuestia (b. ca. 350; d. 428)

Theodore of Mopsuestia was born in Antioch and is sometimes called Theodore of Antioch. He was the Bishop of Mopsuestia in Cilicia, which is now a village called Yakapinar in Turkey. Theodore wrote various scriptural commentaries, including a commentary on the minor prophets of the Old Testament. His scriptural commentaries are representative of the method of interpretation employed in Antioch at that time, the Antiochene school of hermeneutics.

Thomas Aquinas, St. (b. ca. 1225; d. 1274)

Thomas of Aquin, Italy, was a Dominican priest, theologian, and philosopher. His best-known works are the *Summa theologica* (or *Summa theologiae*) and the *Summa contra Gentiles.* Thomas, a Doctor of the Church, is often referred to as the Angelic Doctor because of his insightfrul writings on the angels.

Vianney, John Mary, St. (b. May 8, 1786; d. August 4, 1859)

Jean Marie Baptiste Vianney was a priest in Ars, France, and hence he is also called the "Curé d'Ars." He became famous throughout Europe for his priestly dedication and pastoral work. Vianney engaged in much mortification and often heard confessions for sixteen to eighteen hours a day. Vianney is the patron saint of parish priests.

Zwingli, Ulrich (b. January 1, 1484; d. October 11, 1531)

Ulrich Zwingli led the Protestant Reformation in Switzerland. He was heavily influenced by the writings of Erasmus. Zwingli's first public controversy, in 1522, involved his attacks against the custom of fasting during Lent. He also criticized the use of images and the Mass itself, replacing the latter with a communion liturgy. Zwingli died in battle at the age of forty-seven.

Notes

[1] That is equal to 22 degrees below zero, Fahrenheit.

[2] In his *Dialogues* III , Pope Gregory the Great recounts how Pope Agapitus (535–536) distributed Communion in the mouth.

[3] See J. A. Jungmann, *The Mass of the Roman Rite: Its Origins and Development (Missarum Solemnia)* (Westminster, Md.: Christian Classics, 1986), vol. 2, p. 381.

[4] See Gian Domenico Mansi, *Sacrorum Conciliorum nova et amplissima collectio*, 10:1199–1200.

[5] See *Regula coenobialis*, 9.

[6] See Jungmann, 2:382.

[7] See Jungmann, 2:382.

[8] From the hymn *Sacris Solemniis*, sung at the Office of Readings on the Solemnity of Corpus Christi: *Panis angelicus fit panis hominum. O res mirabilis! Manducat Dominum pauper, servus et humilis.*

[9] *Paedagogus*, I, 42, 3.

[10] *In Ioann. hom.* 82, 5.

[11] See St. Cyprian, *Ad Quirinum*, III, 94; St. Basil the Great, *Regulæ brevius tract.*, 172; St. John Chrysostom., *Hom. Nativ.*, 7.

[12] *De oratione*, 29.

[13] *Enarrationes in Psalmos*, 98, 9: "*Nemo illam carnem manducat, nisi prius adoraverit... peccemus non adorando.*"

[14] *Collectiones canonum Copticae*: Heinrich Denzinger, *Ritus Orientalium* (Würzburg, 1863), vol. 1, p. 405: "*Omnes prosternent se adorantes usque ad terram, parvi et magni incipientque distribuere Communionem.*"

[15] *Catech. Myst.* 5, 22.

[16] *In 1 Cor. hom.* 24, 5.

[17] See Jungmann, 2:377, n. 25.

[18] *The Spirit of the Liturgy* (San Francisco: Ignatius Press, 2000), p. 90.

[19] Ibid., p. 194.

[20] Ibid., p. 185.

[21] See Instruction *Eucharisticum mysterium*, no. 34; Instruction *Inaestimabile donum*, no. 11.

[22] *Ecclesia de Eucharistia*, no. 55

[23] Ibid., no. 62.

[24] *La Madonna e Papa Giovanni* (Catania, 1969), p. 60.

[25] *In 1 Cor. hom.* 24, 5.

[26] *Mystagogical Catecheses*, 5, 2. But a few verses ahead of this citation is the one most frequently used to demonstrate Communion-in-the-hand as a normative practice in the patristic era. This book disputes that point but also shows how, even employing that usage, extraordinary care was exercised in regard to the Eucharistic Species.

[27] *De corona* 3: "*Calicis aut panis aliquid decuti in terram anxie patimur.*"

[28] *In Exod. hom.* 13, 3.

[29] *In Ps.* 147, 14.

[30] *"Deus prohibeat, ne quid ex margaritis seu ex particulis consecratis adhaereat, aut in terram decidat"* (Denzinger, *Ritus Orientalium,* I, p. 95).

[31] *Sermones in Hebdomada Sancta,* 4, 4.

[32] Instruction of the Sacred Congregation for the Discipline of the Sacraments, 26 March 1929: AAS 21 (1920) 635.

[33] Apostolic Letter, *Dominicae Cenae,* 24 February 1980, no. 11.

[34] See *Summa theol.,* III, q. 80, a. 12c.

[35] See *Summa theol.,* III, q. 60, a. 5c, ad 3.

[36] *Christ in His Mysteries* (St. Louis: B. Herder, 1939), pp. 356–357.

[37] Ibid., p. 357.

[38] See St. Athanasius, *Ep. heort,* 5. See also Jungmann, 2:380, n. 43.

[39] See St. Cyprian, *Ep. 58,* 9; St. Cyril of Jerusalem, *Cat. Myst.* 5, 21; St. John Chrysostom, *In 1 Cor. hom.* 25,5; Theodore of Mopsuestia, *Cat. hom.* 16, 27. In the rite of Communion-in-the-hand as it has been practiced in the Roman Rite since around 1968, the Eucharistic Bread is received on the left hand, instead of on the right, as was the norm in antiquity. Furthermore, in the contemporary rite of Communion-in-the-hand, the faithful themselves take the Body of the Lord placed on their hands and then put It into their mouths with their fingers.

[40] This is a reference to the Communion cloth that women presented to receive the Body of the Lord.

[41] *Sermo,* 227, 5.

[42] *Hom. catech.* 16, 27.

[43] Canon of John Bar-Abfgari: *"Sacerdoti praecipit, ut palmis manuum particulam sumat, neve corporis particulam manu ore inferat, sed ore capiat, quia caelestis est cibus"* (Denzinger, vol. 1, p. 81).

[44] See *Church, Ecumenism, Politics: New Essays in Ecclesiology* (New York: Crossroad, 1988), p. 10.

[45] *De sacerdotio,* VI, 4.

[46] *Sermones in Hebdomada Sancta,* 4, 5.

[47] According to the Paleo-Slavic edition: *Bozestwennaya Liturgia Swjatago Apostola Iakowa Brata Boziya I perwago ierarcha Ierusalima* (Roma-Grottaferrata, 1970), p. 91.

[48] *De Fide Orthodoxa,* 4:13.

[49] See Karl Christian Felmy, "Customs and Practices Surrounding Holy Communion in the Eastern Orthodox Churches," in Charles Caspers, ed., *Bread of Heaven: Customs and Practices Surrounding Holy Communion* (Kampen, 1995), pp. 41–59; also, J.-M. Hanssens, "Le Cérémonial de la communion eucharistique dan les rites orientaux," *Gregorianum* 41 (1961): 30–62.

[50] *Feast of Faith: Approaches to a Theology of the Liturgy* (San Francisco: Ignatius Press, 1986), p. 151.

[51] *Hom. in Ps.* 133, 2.

[52] See J. R. Laise, *Comunión en la mano: Documentos e historia* (San Luis, 1997), pp. 68–69.

[53] Congregation for Oriental Churches, Instruction *Il Padre inestimabile* for the application of liturgical prescriptions of the Code of Canons of the Eastern Churches, 6 January 1996, no. 58.

[54] *Spirit of the Liturgy,* p. 194.

[55] *Dominicae Cenae,* no. 8.

[56] See Sacred Congregation for Divine Worship, Instruction *Memoriale Domini*, Enchiridion Vaticanum, III, no. 1273.

[57] "Reverence in Worship," *Parochial and Plain Sermons* (London: Longmans, Green & Co., 1908), 8:5.

[58] *Hom. 82, 6 in Ev. Matt.*

[59] James Meyer, O.F.M., *The Words of St. Francis* (Chicago: Franciscan Herald Press, 1966), p. 175.

[60] *Quemadmodum ex omnibus sacris mysteriis, quae nobis tamquam divinae gratiae certissima instrumenta Dominus Salvator noster commendavit, nullum est quod cum sanctissimo Eucharistiae sacramento comparari queat, ita etiam nulla gravior alicuius sceleris animadversio a Deo metuenda est, quam si res omnis sanctitatis plena, vel potius quae ipsum sanctitatis auctorem et fontem continent, neque sancta neque religiose a fidelibus tractetur.* —In *Catechismus Romanus* [Catechism of the Council of Trent], Pars II, cap. 4.

[61] The *diskos* is the Eastern equivalent of the paten of the Latin Rite.

[62] Text attributed to Narsai of Nisibi (399–502), the theologian *par excellence* of the Nestorian Church. Cited in the Instruction *Il Padre inestimabile.*

[63] *Hom. in Nativ. 7.*

[64] See German translation with critical notes: Nikolay V. Gogol, *Betrachtungen ber die Güttliche Liturgie. Mit einem Beitrag von Prof. Dr. Fairy v. Lilienfeld* (Würzburg, 1989).

[65] Ibid., pp. 105, 110.

[66] See Swajatoj prawednyi Ioann Kronshtadskij, *Moya zisnj wo Christje* (Moscow, 2006), p. 248, n. 444.

[67] In the Byzantine Liturgy, the deacon urges: "Approach with fear of God and with faith."

[68] The editorial council of the Russian Orthodox Church has recently edited the explanation of the Divine Liturgy by the learned bishop Bessarion Neciayew (1828–1905): *Ob 'yasneniye Bozestvennoy Liturgii* (Moscow, 2006), p. 389.

[69] According to an expression of Romano Guardini: "Die erste, immer wieder zu erfahrende Wirkung des Liturgischen is: es löst vom Täglichen ab und befreit." *Vorschule des Betens* (Einsiedeln, 1943), p. 260.

[70] J. R. Luth, "Communion in the Churches of the Dutch Reformation to the Present Day," in Charles Caspers, ed., *Bread of Heaven*, p. 101.

[71] Ibid.

[72] Ibid., p. 108.

[73] A. Heinz, "Liturgical Roles and Popular Religious Customs Surrounding Holy Communion between the Council of Trent and the Catholic Restoration of the Nineteenth Century," in Caspers, *Bread of Heaven*, pp. 137–138.

[74] The article appeared in the review *Humanitas* 20 (1965) and is cited in R. Tagliferi, *La "magia" del rito. Saggi sulla questione rituale e liturgica* (Padova, 2006), p. 406.

[75] John Edward Bowden, *The Life and Letters of Frederick William Faber, D.D.* (London: Thomas Richardson and Son, 1869), p. 191.

[76] From the Vulgate, when the disciples recognized the Risen Lord, Jn 21:7.

p 34 + 43
37